Motivational Quotes

365 days of the best motivational quotes

Table of Contents

Introduction 1

365 Motivational Quotes 2

Conclusion 124

Introduction

Thank you for choosing this book, containing 365 motivational quotes.

In the following pages, you will find a collection of the most inspiring and motivating quotes. There are quotes from a wide variety of people, from ancient philosophers, to athletes, to activists!

With this book, you can choose to either read one new quote every day for the next year, or simply open to a random page whenever you feel the need.

No matter how you choose to use this book, I hope that the quotes within can encourage and motivate you to pursue your dreams, focus on the good, and live a fulfilled and happy life! Enjoy!

365 Motivational Quotes

1.

"All our dreams can come true, if we have the courage to pursue them."

- Walt Disney

2.

"If people are doubting how far you can go, go so far that you can't hear them anymore."

- Michele Ruiz

3.

"It's hard to beat a person who never gives up."

- Babe Ruth

4.

"Write it. Shoot it. Publish it. Crochet it, sauté it, whatever. MAKE."

- Joss Whedon

5.

"Everything you can imagine is real."

- Pablo Picasso

6.

"Do one thing every day that scares you."

- Eleanor Roosevelt

7.

"Fairy tales are more than true: not because they tell us that dragons exist, but because they tell us that dragons can be beaten."

- Neil Gaiman

8.

"Intelligent individuals learn from everything and everyone; average people, from their experiences. The stupid already have all the answers."

- Socrates

9.

"Do what you feel in your heart to be right – for you'll be criticized anyway."

- Eleanor Roosevelt

10.

"Whatever you are, be a good one."

- Abraham Lincoln

11.

"Happiness is not something ready-made. It comes from your own actions."

- Dalai Lama XIV

12.

"Failure is a bruise, not a tattoo."

- Jon Sinclair

13.

"Do what you have to do until you can do what you want to do."

- Oprah Winfrey

14.

"Work like there is someone working twenty-four hours a day to take it away from you."

- Mark Cuban

15.

"Find something you're passionate about and keep tremendously interested in it."

- Julia Child

16.

"You can't solve a problem on the same level it was created. You have to rise above it to the next level."

- Albert Einstein

17.

"Be in love with your life. Every minute of it."

- Jack Kerouac

18.

"Elegance is not about being noticed, it's about being remembered."

- Giorgio Armani

19.

"Always be a work in progress."

- Emily Lillian

20.

"You can, you should, and if you're brave enough to start, you will."

- Stephen King

21.

"Attitude is the difference between an ordeal and an adventure."

- Bob Bitchin

22.

"The same boiling water that softens the potato hardens the egg. It's what you're made of. Not the circumstances."

- Unknown

23.

"You can either experience the pain of discipline or the pain of regret. The choice is yours."

- Unknown

24.

"Impossible is just an opinion."

- Paulo Coelho

25.

"Your passion is waiting for your courage to catch up."

- Isabelle Lafleche

26.

"If something is important enough, even if the odds are stacked against you, you should still do it."

- Elon Musk

27.

"Hold the vision. Trust the process."

- Unknown

28.

"Don't be afraid to give up the good to go for the great."

- John D. Rockefeller

29.

"One day or day one. You decide."

- Unknown

30.

"No one is to blame for your future situation but yourself. If you want to be successful, then become successful."

- Jaymin Shah

31.

"Tend to your vital heart, and all that you worry about will be solved."

- Rumi

32.

"Always remember to fall asleep with a dream and wake up with a purpose."

- Unknown

33.

"The first wealth is health."

- Ralph Waldo Emerson

34.

"Do what you have to do until you can do what you want to do."

- Oprah Winfrey

35.

"Whenever you see a successful business, someone made a courageous decision."

- Peter Drucker

36.

"Be in love with your life. Every minute of it."

- Jack Kerouac

37.

"Always be a work in progress."

- Emily Lillian

38.

"Work hard in silence. Let your success be your noise."

- Frank Ocean

39.

"We are what we repeatedly do. Excellence, then, is not an act, but a habit."

- Aristotle

40.

"How wonderful is it that nobody need wait a single moment before starting to improve the world."

- Anne Frank

41.

"Some people want it to happen, some wish it would happen, others make it happen."

- Michael Jordan

42.

"Great things are done by a series of small things brought together."

- Vincent Van Gogh

43.

"Very often, a change of self is needed more than a change of scene."

- A.C. Benson

44.

"It's not the load that breaks you down, it's the way you carry it."

- Lou Holtz

45.

"The hard days are what make you stronger."

- Aly Raisman

46.

"If you believe it'll work out, you'll see opportunities. If you don't believe it'll work out, you'll see obstacles."

- Wayne Dyer

47.

"In a gentle way, you can shake the world."

- Mahatma Gandhi

48.

"Keep your eyes on the stars, and your feet on the ground."

- Theodore Roosevelt

49.

"You've got to get up every morning with determination if you're going to go to bed with satisfaction."

- George Lorimer

50.

"If opportunity doesn't knock, build a door."

- Kurt Cobain

51.

"Don't be pushed around by the fears in your mind. Be led by the dreams in your heart."

- Roy T. Bennett

52.

"Mistakes are proof that you're trying."

- Unknown

53.

"Don't say you don't have enough time. You have the exact same number of hours per day that were given to Hellen Keller, Pasteur, Michelangelo, Mother Teresa, Leonardo Da Vinci, Thomas Jefferson, and Albert Einstein."

- H. Jackson Brown Jr.

54.

"Hard work beats talent when talent doesn't work hard."

- Tim Notke

55.

"Do something today that your future self will thank you for."

- Unknown

56.

"Opportunity is missed by most people because it is dressed in overalls and looks like work."

- Thomas Edison

57.

"If everything seems to be under control, you're not going fast enough."

- Mario Andretti

58.

"The only difference between ordinary and extraordinary is that little extra."

- Jimmy Johnson

59.

"Sometimes when you're in a dark place, you think you've been buried, but actually you've been planted."

- Unknown

60.

"Work hard, be kind, and amazing things will happen."

- Conan O'Brien

61.

"Never stop doing your best just because someone doesn't give you credit."

- Kamari aka Lyrikal

62.

"Whatever you decide to do, make sure it makes you happy."

- Unknown

63.

"Unsuccessful people make decisions based on their current situations. Successful people make decisions based on where they want to be."

- Benjamin Hardy

64.

"Never give up on a dream just because of the time it will take to accomplish it. The time will pass anyway."

- Earl Nightingale

65.

"If you cannot do great things, do smalls things in a great way."

- Napoleon Hill

66.

"Start each day with a positive thought."

- Unknown

67.

"Amateurs sit around and wait for inspiration. The rest of us get up and go to work."

- Stephen King

68.

"The big secret in life is that there is no secret. Whatever your goal, you can get there if you're willing to work."

- Oprah Winfrey

69.

"Nothing will work unless you do."

- Maya Angelou

70.

"Trust the vibes you get, energy doesn't lie."

- Unknown

71.

"Don't limit your challenges. Challenge your limits."

- Unknown

72.

"We know what we are, but know not what we may be."

- William Shakespeare

73.

"Whenever you find yourself doubting how far you can go, just remember how far you have come."

- Unknown

74.

"In the middle of every difficulty lies opportunity."

- Albert Einstein

75.

"Try to be a rainbow is someone's cloud."

- Maya Angelou

76.

"Find something you're passionate about and keep tremendously interested in it."

- Julia Child

77.

"Don't quit yet. The worst moments are usually followed by the most beautiful silver linings. You have to stay strong, remember to keep your head up and remain hopeful."

- Unknown

78.

"When written in Chinese, the word "crisis" is composed of two characters – one represents danger and the other represents opportunity."

- John F. Kennedy

79.

"Good, better, best. Never let it rest, until your good is better and your better is best."

- St. Jerome

80.

"Do your little bit of good where you are; it's those little bits of good put together that overwhelm the world."

- Desmond Tutu

81.

"I hated every minute of training, but I said, "Don't quit. Suffer now and live the rest of your life as a champion."

- Muhammad Ali

82.

"If opportunity doesn't knock, build a door."

- Unknown

83.

"In the middle of every difficulty lies opportunity."

- Albert Einstein

84.

"Start where you are. Use what you have. Do what you can."

- Arthur Ashe

85.

"Dreams don't work unless you do."

- John C. Maxwell

86.

"It is during our darkest moments that we must focus to see the light."

- Aristotle

87.

"The power of imagination makes us infinite."

- John Muir

88.

"The best way out is always through."

- Robert Frost

89.

"Make each day your masterpiece."

- John Wooden

90.

"Be fearless in the pursuit of what sets your soul on fire."

- Unknown

91.

"Your present circumstances don't determine where you can go; they merely determine where you start."

- Nido Qubein

92.

"With self-discipline, most anything is possible."

- Theodore Roosevelt

93.

"Just don't give up trying to do what you really want to do. Where there is love and inspiration, I don't think you can go wrong."

- Ella Fitzgerald

94.

"Go the extra mile. It's never crowded there."
- Dr. Wayne D. Dyer

95.

"Turn your wounds into wisdom."
- Oprah Winfrey

96.

"Wherever you go, go with all your heart."
- Confucius

97.

"If a man does not keep pace with his companions, perhaps it is because he hears a different drummer. Let him step to the music which he hears, however measured or far away."

- Henry David Thoreau

98.

"No matter what people tell you, words and ideas can change the world."

- Robin Williams

99.

"Cherish your visions and your dreams as they are the children of your soul, the blueprints of your ultimate achievements."

- Napoleon Hill

100.

"If you accept the expectations of others, especially negative ones, then you never will change the outcome."

- Michael Jordan

101.

"Begin anywhere."

- John Cage

102.

"Success is no accident. It is hard work, perseverance, learning, studying, sacrifice and most of all, love of what you are doing or learning to do."

- Pele

103.

"Every champion was once a contender that didn't give up."

- Gabby Douglas

104.

"Big things often have small beginnings."

- Unknown

105.

"Someone is sitting in the shade today because someone planted a tree a long time ago."

- Warren Buffett

106.

"Happiness is not something you postpone for the future; it is something you design for the present."

- Jim Rohn

107.

"Opportunities don't happen. You create them."

- Chris Grosser

108.

"You can cry, scream, and bang your head in frustration, but keep pushing forward. It's worth it."

- Unknown

109.

"Success is liking yourself, liking what you do, and liking how you do it."

- Maya Angelou

110.

"What you do today can improve all your tomorrows."

- Unknown

111.

"There is nothing impossible to him who will try."

- Alexander the Great

112.

"We can change our lives. We can do, have, and be exactly what we wish."

- Tony Robbins

113.

"I believe every human has a finite number of heartbeats. I don't intend to waste any of mine."

- Neil Armstrong

114.

"You don't need a new day to start over, you only need a new mindset."

- Hazel Hira Ozbek

115.

"Never regret anything that made you smile."

- Mark Twain

116.

"If you want to fly, give up everything that weighs you down."

- Buddha

117.

"It is never too late to be what you might have been."

- George Eliot

118.

"One today is worth two tomorrows."

- Benjamin Franklin

119.

"What seems to us as bitter trials are often blessings in disguise."

- Oscar Wilde

120.

"Doubt kills more dreams than failure ever will."

- Suzy Kassem

121.

"I never lose. Either I win or learn."

- Nelson Mandela

122.

"You must do the thing you think you cannot do."

- Eleanor Roosevelt

123.

"Today is your opportunity to build the tomorrow you want."

- Ken Poirot

124.

"Live your beliefs and you can turn the world around."

- Henry David Thoreau

125.

"To the mind that is still, the whole universe surrenders."

- Lao Tzu

126.

"We have to choose joy and keep choosing it."

- Henri J.M. Nouwen

127.

"The man who moves a mountain begins by carrying away small stones."

- Confucius

128.

"If you are always trying to be normal you will never know how amazing you can be."

- Maya Angelou

129.

"We are what we repeatedly do."

- Aristotle

130.

"What you do today is important because you are exchanging a day of your life for it."

- Unknown

131.

"Your big opportunity may be right where you are now."

- Napoleon Hill

132.

"Each day provides its own gifts."

- Marcus Aurelius

133.

"Getting over a painful experience is much like crossing the monkey bars. You have to let go at some point in order to move forward."

- C.S. Lewis

134.

"Focus on being productive instead of busy."

- Tim Ferriss

135.

"You don't need to see the whole staircase, just take the first step."

- Martin Luther King Jr.

136.

"Don't tell people your dreams – show them."

- Unknown

137.

"Look within. Within is the fountain of good, and it will ever bubble up, if thou wilt ever dig."

- Marcus Aurelius

138.

"When someone says you can't do it, do it twice and take pictures."

- Unknown

139.

"I didn't get there by wishing for it, but by working for it."

- Estee Lauder

140.

"The big lesson in life is never be scared of anyone or anything."

- Frank Sinatra

141.

"A goal is not always meant to be reached. It often simply serves as something to aim at."

- Bruce Lee

142.

"Whatever the problem, be part of the solution. Don't just sit around raising questions and pointing out obstacles."

- Tina Fey

143.

"You can't do anything about the length of your life, but you can do something about its width and depth."

- Evan Esar

144.

"Nothing is worth more than this day."

- Johann Wolfgang von Goethe

145.

"Accept the things to which fate binds you, and love the people with whom fate brings you together, but do so with all your heart."

- Marcus Aurelius

146.

"When you can't find the sunshine, be the sunshine."

- Unknown

147.

"If you're too comfortable, it's time to move on. Terrified of what's next? You're on the right track."

- Susan Fales-Hill

148.

"Sunshine all the time makes a desert."

- Arabic Proverb

149.

"If they don't know you personally, don't take it personal."

- Unknown

150.

"The one who falls and gets up is so much stronger than the one who never fell."

- Unknown

151.

"Be so good they can't ignore you."

- Steve Martin

152.

"This is a reminder to create your own rule book, and live your life the way you want it."

- Reese Evans

153.

"I choose to make the rest of my life, the best of my life."

- Louise Hay

154.

"Believe you can and you're halfway there."

- Theodore Roosevelt

155.

"What we think, we become."

- Buddha

156.

"The true sign of intelligence is not knowledge, but imagination."

- Albert Einstein

157.

"Courage is knowing what not to fear."

- Plato

158.

"We are only as blind as we want to be."

- Maya Angelou

159.

"You don't have a soul. You are a soul. You have a body."

- C.S. Lewis

160.

"Today is the only day. Yesterday is gone."

- John Wooden

161.

"Shoot for the moon and if you miss you will still be among the stars."

- Les Brown

162.

"If you can dream it, you can do it."

- Walt Disney

163.

"Don't let what you can't do interfere with what you can do."

- Unknown

164.

"You can do anything you set your mind to."

- Benjamin Franklin

165.

"Small changes eventually add up to huge results."

- Unknown

166.

"Life goes by fast. Enjoy it. Calm down. It's all funny."

- Joan Rivers

167.

"We have it in our power to begin the world over again."

- Thomas Paine

168.

"Your ordinary acts of love and hope point to the extraordinary promise that every human life is of inestimable value."

- Desmond Tutu

169.

"Nothing is impossible. The word itself says 'I'm Possible'."

- Audrey Hepburn

170.

"The best time for new beginnings is now."

- Unknown

171.

"If we did all the things we are capable of, we would literally astound ourselves."

- Thomas A. Edison

172.

"Men must live and create. Live to the point of tears."

- Albert Camus

173.

"All we can do is the best we can do."

- David Axelrod

174.

"Twenty years from now you'll be more disappointed by the things you did not do than the ones you did."

- Mark Twain

175.

"Trust yourself that you can do it and get it."

- Baz Luhrmann

176.

"You never know what you can do until you try."

- William Cobbett

177.

"Never let your fear decide your future."

- Unknown

178.

"If the doors of perception were cleansed, everything would appear to man as it is, infinite."

- William Blake

179.

"Even if I knew that tomorrow the world would go to pieces, I would still plant my apple tree."

- Martin Luther King Jr.

180.

"The only journey is the one within."

- Rainer Maria Rilke

181.

"It is okay to outgrow people who don't grow. Grow tall anyways."

- Unknown

182.

"The world is full of nice people. If you can't find one, be one."

- Nishan Panwar

183.

"Your only limit is you."

- Unknown

184.

"Vitality shows in not only the ability to persist, but the ability to start over."

- F. Scott Fitzgerald

185.

"Noble deeds that are concealed are most esteemed."

- Blaise Pascal

186.

"God loves to help him who strives to help himself."

- Aeschylus

187.

"The fact that you aren't where you want to be, should be enough motivation."

- Unknown

188.

"Believe in yourself, take on your challenges, dig deep within yourself to conquer fears. Never let anyone bring you down. You've got to keep going."

- Chantal Sutherland

189.

"I can and I will. Watch me."

- Carrie Green

190.

"If you can't do anything about it, then let it go. Don't be a prisoner to things you can't change."

- Tony Gaskins

191.

"Yesterday I was clever, so I wanted to change the world. Today I am wise, so I am changing myself."

- Rumi

192.

"There are only two options: Make progress or make excuses."

- Unknown

193.

"Do not judge me by my successes, judge me by how many times I fell down and got back up again."

- Nelson Mandela

194.

"From a small seed a tiny trunk may grow."

- Aeschylus

195.

"Nurture your minds with great thoughts. To believe in the heroic makes heroes."

- Benjamin Disraeli

196.

"If you don't have big dreams & goals, you'll end up working really hard for someone who does."

- Unknown

197.

"The only thing standing in the way between you and your goal is the BS story you keep telling yourself as to why you can't achieve it."

- Jordan Belfort

198.

"I attribute my success to this: I never gave or took an excuse."

- Florence Nightingale

199.

"What is life without a little risk?"

- J.K. Rowling

200.

"Only do what your heart tells you."

- Princess Diana

201.

"If it's a good idea, go ahead and do it. It's much easier to apologize than it is to get permission."

- Grace Hopper

202.

"The question isn't who is going to let me; it's who is going to stop me."

- Ayn Rand

203.

"The best way to predict the future is to create it."

- Peter Drucker

204.

"Take time to do what makes your soul happy"

- Unknown

205.

"And above all things, never think that you're not good enough yourself. A man should never think that. My belief is that in life people will take you at your own reckoning."

- Isaac Asimov

206.

"What we achieve inwardly will change outer reality."

- Plutarch

207.

"I will love the light for it shows me the way, yet I will endure the darkness because it shows me the stars."

- Og Mandino

208.

"It seems to me we can never give up longing and wishing while we are thoroughly alive. There are certain things we feel to be beautiful and good, and we must hunger after them."

- George Eliot

209.

"You are what you do, not what you say you'll do."

- Unknown

210.

"I am deliberate and afraid of nothing."

- Audre Lorde

211.

"Only those who have learned the power of sincere and selfless contribution experience life's deepest joy: true fulfillment."

- Tony Robbins

212.

"The best preparation for tomorrow is doing your best today."

- H. Jackson Brown Jr.

213.

"A surplus of effort could overcome a deficit of confidence."

- Sonia Sotomayer

214.

"And, when you want something, all the universe conspires in helping you to achieve it."

- Paulo Coelho

215.

"I can be changed by what happens to me. But I refuse to be reduced by it."

- Maya Angelou

216.

"Darkness cannot drive out darkness; only light can do that. Hate cannot drive out hate; only love can do that."

- Martin Luther King Jr.

217.

"Follow your soul. It knows the way."

- Unknown

218.

"No amount of security is worth the suffering of a mediocre life chained to a routine that had killed your dreams."

- Maya Mendoza

219.

"All progress takes place outside the comfort zone."

- Unknown

220.

"It is in your moments of decision that your destiny is shaped."

- Tony Robbins

221.

"You are always free to change your mind and choose a different future, or a different past."

- Richard Bach

222.

"It's the possibility of having a dream come true that makes life interesting."

- Paulo Coelho

223.

"Learn to light a candle in the darkest moments of someone's life. Be the light that helps others see; it is what gives life its deepest significance."

- Roy T. Bennett

224.

"On my own I will just create and if it works, it works. And if it doesn't, I'll just create something else. I don't have any limitations on what I think I could do or be."

- Oprah Winfrey

225.

"We need to accept that we won't always make the right decisions, that we'll screw up royally sometimes – understanding that failure is not the opposite of success, it's part of success."

- Arianna Huffington

226.

"Forget the mistake. Remember the lesson."

- Unknown

227.

"Grow through what you go through."

- Unknown

228.

"The meaning I picked, the one that changed my life: Overcome fear, behold wonder."

- Richard Bach

229.

"Let every dawn be to you as the beginning of life, and every setting sun be to you as its close."

- John Ruskin

230.

"Let us sacrifice our today so that our children can have a better tomorrow."

- A. P. J. Abdul Kalam

231.

"Be so good they can't ignore you."

- Steve Martin

232.

"Wealth is not about having a lot of money, it's about having a lot of options."

- Chris Rock

233.

"When you think about quitting, think about why you started."

- Unknown

234.

"I believe that one defines oneself by reinvention. To not be like your parents. To not be like your friends. To be yourself. To cut yourself out of stone."

- Henry Rollins

235.

"I can't change the direction of the wind, but I can adjust my sails to always reach my destination."

- Jimmy Dean

236.

"Change your thoughts and you change your world."

- Norman Vincent Peale

237.

"Don't compromise yourself. You're all you've got."

- Janis Joplin

238.

"When something I can't control happens, I ask myself: Where is the hidden gift? Where is the positive in this?"

- Sara Blakely

239.

"Doubt is a killer. You have to know who you are and what you stand for."

- Jennifer Lopez

240.

"Ambition is the first step to success. The second step is action."

- Unknown

241.

"If you don't sacrifice for what you want, then what you want becomes the sacrifice."

- Unknown

242.

"Learn from the mistakes of others. You can't live long enough to make them all yourself."

- Eleanor Roosevelt

243.

"Done is better than perfect."

- Sheryl Sandberg

244.

"Once we believe in ourselves, we can risk curiosity, wonder, spontaneous delight, or any experience that reveals the human spirit."

- E. E. Cummings

245.

"If you believe in yourself and have dedication and pride – and never quit, you'll be a winner. The price of victory is high, but so are the rewards."

- Bear Bryant

246.

"Give light, and the darkness will disappear of itself."

- Desiderius Erasmus

247.

"If your dreams don't scare you, they are too small."

- Richard Branson

248.

"What hurts you, blesses you."

- Rumi

249.

"I always thought it was me against the world, and then one day I realized it's just me against me."

- Kendrick Lamar

250.

"Don't be pushed by your problems. Be led by your dreams."

- Ralph Waldo Emerson

251.

"Throw your dreams into space like a kite, and you do not know what it will bring back, a new life, a new friend, a new love, a new country."

- Anais Nin

252.

"Great hopes make great men."

- Thomas Fuller

253.

"A man is not finished when he is defeated. He is finished when he quits."

- Richard Nixon

254.

"The world is changed by your example, not by your opinion."

- Paulo Coelho

255.

"Dream beautiful dreams, and then work to make those dreams come true."

- Spencer W. Kimball

256.

"The expert in anything was once a beginner."

- Unknown

257.

"Attract what you expect. Reflect what you desire. Become what you respect. Mirror what you admire."

- Unknown

258.

"What great thing would you attempt if you knew you could not fail?"

- Robert H. Schuller

259.

"Don't limit yourself. Many people limit themselves to what they think they can do. You can go as far as your mind lets you. What you believe, remember, you can achieve."

- Mary Kay Ash

260.

"I have always believed, and I still believe, that whatever good or bad fortune may come our way we can always give it meaning and transform it into something of value."

- Hermann Hesse

261.

"The only way to discover the limits of the possible is to go beyond them into the impossible."

- Arthur C. Clarke

262.

"Be faithful to that which exists in yourself."

- Andre Gide

263.

"I believe that if one always looked at the skies, one would end up with wings."

- Gustave Flaubert

264.

"There is a loftier ambition than merely to stand high in the world. It is to stoop down and lift mankind a little higher."

- Henry Van Dyke

265.

"Be the change you want to see in the world."
- Mahatma Gandhi

266.

"Be silly, be honest, be kind."
- Ralph Waldo Emerson

267.

"Your value doesn't decrease based on someone's inability to see your worth."
- Unknown

268.

"It's not what happens to you but how you react to it that matters."

- Epictetus

269.

"You don't have to be perfect to be amazing."

- Unknown

270.

"The best way to predict your future is to create it."

- Abraham Lincoln

271.

"Successful people are not gifted, they just work hard, then succeed on purpose."

- G.K. Nielson

272.

"You have been criticizing yourself for years, and it hasn't worked. Try approving of yourself and see what happens."

- Louise L. Hay

273.

"Someone once told me not to bite off more than I could chew. I said: I'd rather choke on greatness than nibble on mediocrity."

- Unknown

274.

"Light tomorrow with today!"

- Elizabeth Barrett Browning

275.

"Let us make our future now, and let us make our dreams tomorrow's reality."

- Malala Yousafzai

276.

"For a gallant spirit there can never be defeat."

- Wallis Simpson

277.

"Whatever you vividly imagine, ardently desire, sincerely believe, and enthusiastically act upon… must inevitably come to pass!"

- Paul J. Meyer

278.

"Happiness resides not in possessions, and not in gold, happiness dwells in the soul."

- Democritus

279.

"Don't watch the clock; do what it does. Keep going."

- Sam Levenson

280.

"Falling down is how we grow. Staying down is how we die."

- Brian Vaszily

281.

"There may be people that have more talent than you, but there's no excuse for anyone to work harder than you."

- Derek Jeter

282.

"When you know your worth, no one can make you feel worthless."

- Unknown

283.

"If you judge people, you have no time to love them."

- Mother Teresa

284.

"What is done in love is done well."

- Vincent Van Gogh

285.

"Rule your mind or it will rule you."

- Buddha

286.

"If the plan doesn't work, change the plan, but never the goal."

- Unknown

287.

"I believe there's an inner power than makes winners or losers. And the winners are the ones who really listen to the truth of their hearts."

- Sylvester Stallone

288.

"Ideas shape the course of history."

- John Maynard Keynes

289.

"The authentic self is the soul made visible."

- Sarah Ban Breathnach

290.

"A champion is someone who gets up when he can't."

- Jack Dempsey

291.

"Be brave enough to live life creatively. The creative place where no one else has ever been."

- Alan Alda

292.

"Create each day anew."

- Morihei Ueshiba

293.

"Happiness is the natural flower of duty."

- Phillips Brooks

294.

"Put your heart, mind, and soul into even your smallest acts. This is the secret of success."

- Swami Sivananda

295.

"Man never made any material as resilient as the human spirit."

- Bernard Williams

296.

"The two most important days in your life are the day you're born and the day you find out why."

- Mark Twain

297.

"Nothing ever goes away until it teaches us what we need to know."

- Pema Chodron

298.

"Always remember to fall asleep with a dream and wake up with a purpose."

- Unknown

299.

"Enthusiasm moves the world."

- Arthur Balfour

300.

"Let each man exercise the art he knows."

- Aristophanes

301.

"You don't get paid for the hour. You get paid for the value you bring to the hour."

- Jim Rohn

302.

"Be an Encourager: When you encourage others, you boost their self-esteem, enhance their self-confidence, make them work harder, lift their spirits and make them successful in their endeavors. Encouragement goes straight to the heart and is always available. Be an Encourager. Always."

- Roy T. Bennett

303.

"Go the extra mile. It's never crowded."

- Unknown

304.

"Learn the rules like a pro, so you can break them like an artist."

- Pablo Picasso

305.

"When you have a bad day, a really bad day, try and treat the world better than it treated you."

- Patrick Stump

306.

"Always look on the bright side of life."

- Unknown

307.

"Find out who you are and be that person. That's what your soul was put on this Earth to be. Find that truth, live that truth and everything else will come."

- Ellen DeGeneres

308.

"Everything you want is out there waiting for you to ask. Everything you want also wants you. But you have to take action to get it."

- Jules Renard

309.

"Wonder, rather than doubt, is the root of all knowledge."

- Abraham Joshua Heschel

310.

"Try to be like the turtle – at ease in your own shell."

- Bill Copeland

311.

"What we need is more people who specialize in the impossible."

- Theodore Roethke

312.

"Out of difficulties grow miracles."

- Jean de la Bruyere

313.

"I believe in living today. Not in yesterday, nor in tomorrow."

- Loretta Young

314.

"Work hard and don't give up hope. Be open to criticism and keep learning. Surround yourself with happy, warm, and genuine people."

- Tena Desae

315.

"You can control two things: your work ethic and your attitude about anything."

- Ali Krieger

316.

"Success isn't always about greatness. It's about consistency. Consistent hard work leads to success. Greatness will come."

- Dwayne Johnson

317.

"I really appreciate people who correct me, because without them, I might have been repeating mistakes for a long time."

- Mufti Menk

318.

"Motivation comes from working on things we care about."

- Sheryl Sandberg

319.

"If today you are a little bit better than you were yesterday, then that's enough."

- David A. Bednar

320.

"Education is the most powerful weapon which you can use to change the world."

- Nelson Mandela

321.

"Don't ever doubt your worth."

- Unknown

322.

"It is always the simple that produces the marvelous."
- Amelia Barr

323.

"Reach for the stars."
- Christa McAuliffe

324.

"The undertaking of a new action brings new strength."
- Richard L. Evans

325.

"Memories of our lives, of our works and our deeds will continue in others."

- Rosa Parks

326.

"Today I choose life. Every morning when I wake up I can choose joy, happiness, negativity, pain… To feel the freedom that comes from being able to continue to make mistakes and choices – today I choose to feel life, not to deny my humanity but embrace it."

- Kevyn Aucoin

327.

"From its brilliancy everything is illuminated."

- Guru Nanak

328.

"If you can't make a mistake, you can't make anything."

- Marva Collin

329.

"You may be disappointed if you fail, but you'll be doomed if you don't try."

- Beverly Sills

330.

"Failure is the tuition you pay for success."

- Walter Brunell

331.

"If we wait until we're ready, we'll be waiting for the rest of our lives."

- Lemony Snicket

332.

"Study while others are sleeping; work while others are loafing; prepare while others are playing; and dream while others are wishing."

- William Arthur Ward

333.

"It always seems impossible until it's done."

- Unknown

334.

"Happiness is when what you think, what you say, and what you do are in harmony."

- Mahatma Gandhi

335.

"I have found that most people are about as happy as they make their minds up to be."

- Abraham Lincoln

336.

"You are allowed to be both a masterpiece and a work in progress, simultaneously."

- Sophia Bush

337.

"Success is 99.9% an inside job."

- Emily Williams

338.

"I don't want other people to decide who I am. I want to decide that for myself."

- Emma Watson

339.

"Be somebody who makes everybody feel like somebody."

- Unknown

340.

"The most authentic thing about us is our capacity to create, to overcome, to endure, to transform, to love and to be greater than our suffering."

- Ben Okri

341.

"I am not afraid of tomorrow, for I have seen yesterday and I love today."

- William Allen White

342.

"Our ideals are our better selves."

- Amos Bronson Alcott

343.

"I arise full of eagerness and energy, knowing well what achievement lies ahead of me."

- Zane Grey

344.

"If you could only love enough, you could be the most powerful person in the world."

- Emmet Fox

345.

"People tell you the world looks a certain way. Parents tell you how to think. Schools tell you how to think. TV. Religion. And then at a certain point, if you're lucky, you realize you can make up your own mind. Nobody sets the rules but you. You can design your own life."

- Carrie-Anne Moss

346.

"Hope is but the dream of those who wake."

- Matthew Prior

347.

"The best revenge is massive success."

- Frank Sinatra

348.

"If there is no wind, row."

- Latin Proverb

349.

"A goal is a dream with a deadline."

- Napoleon Hill

350.

"Never doubt that a small group of thoughtful, committed citizens can change the world. Indeed, it is the only thing that ever has."

- Margaret Mead

351.

"Change is painful, but nothing is as painful as staying stuck somewhere you don't belong."

- Mandy Hale

352.

"As knowledge increases, wonder deepens."

- Charles Morgan

353.

"If the world seems cold to you, kindle fires to warm it."

- Lucy Larcom

354.

"Thought is the wind, knowledge the sail, and mankind the vessel."

- Augustus Hare

355.

"When deeds speak, words are nothing."

- Pierre-Joseph Proudhon

356.

"Everyone thinks of changing the world, but no one thinks of changing himself."

- Leo Tolstoy

357.

"Change is the law of life. And those who look only to the past or present are certain to miss the future."

- John F. Kennedy

358.

"We delight in the beauty of the butterfly, but rarely admit the changes it has gone through to achieve that beauty."

- Maya Angelou

359.

"Keep your feet on the ground, but let your heart soar as high as it will. Refuse to be average or surrender to the chill of your spiritual environment."

- Arthur Helps

360.

"Somewhere, something incredible is waiting to be known."

- Sharon Begley

361.

"Dreams are the seeds of change. Nothing ever grows without a seed, and nothing ever changes without a dream."

- Debby Boone

362.

"That man is richest who's pleasures are cheapest."

- Henry David Thoreau

363.

"Don't give up, don't take anything personally, and don't take no for an answer."

- Sophia Amoruso

364.

"The secret of change is to focus all your energy, not on fighting the old, but on building the new."

- Socrates

365.

"Your positive action combined with positive thinking results in success."

- Shiv Khera

Conclusion

Thanks again for taking the time to read the quotes contained within this book!

I hope that you were able to draw great motivation from the quotes, and that they have spurred you on to pursue your goals and dreams.

Finally, if you enjoyed the quotes contained within, don't forget to share the love by recommending (or gifting) this book to a friend!

www.ingramcontent.com/pod-product-compliance
Lightning Source LLC
LaVergne TN
LVHW011721060526
838200LV00051B/2980